# The Joke Book

# The Joke Book

## A book
### of
## 1000 laughs

compiled by
## Max Edwards

ARCTURUS

Published by Arcturus Publishing Limited
For Bookmart Limited
Registered Number 2372865
Trading as Bookmart Limited
Desford Road
Enderby
Leicester
LE9 5AD

This edition published 1996

Printed and bound in Great Britain

ISBN1 900032 21 X

What happens when pigs fly?

**The price of bacon goes up.**

❑❑❑❑

Why did the tap dancer have to retire?

**He kept falling in the sink.**

**Please blow into this, sir...**

Heard about the man who was hit on the head with a pan full of curry?

**He ended up in a koorma!**

❑❑❑❑

There were two Bishops in a bed.

Which one wore the nightie?

**Mrs. Bishop.**

## Real life laughs

A capsized boat was spotted near the Pacific coast of the Soviet Union. The only survivor told his rescuers: "A cow fell into our boat." The poor man stuck to his story and was sent to a mental hospital. It was later discovered that an aircraft crew, about to fly from one air base to another, saw a stray cow. Worrying about food, they decided to take her along with them, and drove the unfortunate animal into the plane via the bomb bay. When they rose to a cruising altitude the cow became agitated due to the cold. The crew opened the bomb bay and threw her into the sea, where she landed on the boat.

# WHAT A Joke

If a red house is made of red bricks, and a blue house is made of blue bricks, what's a green house made of?

**Glass.**

□□□□

What do you give a sick pig?

**Oinkment.**

What's the difference between a nail and a bad boxer?

**One's knocked in and the other's knocked out.**

□□□□

Did you know Davy Crockett had three ears?

**A right ear, a left ear and a wild frontier.**

What did the policeman say to his tummy?
**You're under a vest.**

What's short, green and goes camping?
**A boy sprout.**

Knock, knock!
*Who's there?*
Little old lady.
*Little old lady who?*

**I didn't know you could yodel.**

How did the monkey make toast?

**He put it under the gorilla.**

What do jelly babies wear in the rain?

**Gum boots.**

How do you make an apple puff?

**Chase it round the garden.**

**I think you should call it a day. But I'm only the window cleaner...**

2

Doctor, doctor, what can I do, my little boy has swallowed my pen?

**Use a pencil till I get there.**

❑❑❑❑

What's got teeth but can't bite?

**A comb.**

**If you ask me, the ref's losing control of this game...**

What does a Swedish Fred Flintstone say?

**Abba dabba doo!**

What do you get when you cross a jelly with a sheep dog?

**Collie-wobbles.**

What kind of ears does a train have?

**Engineers.**

Max: One of my ancestors died at Waterloo.

**Tom: Really? Which platform?**

Why is a farmer cruel?

**Because he pulls the corn by its ears.**

**We loved Britain - it rained every day**

**WHAT A Joke**

Sam: Do you notice any change in me?

Mum: **No. Why?**

Sam: I just swallowed 5p.

Why couldn't the butterfly get into the dance?

**Because it was a moth-ball.**

◻◻◻◻

Why did the orange stop halfway up the hill?

**Because it ran out of juice.**

What man claps at Christmas?

**Santaplause.**

◻◻◻◻

Why was the farmer cross?

**Because someone trod on his corn.**

◻◻◻◻

How do you use an Egyptian door-bell?

**Toot-and-come-in.**

How do you know when there's an elephant under your bed?

**Your nose touches the ceiling.**

Waiter, waiter, what do you call this?

It's bean soup, sir.

**I don't care what it's been — what is it now?**

Shall I tell you the joke about the butter?

**I'd better not. You'll only spread it.**

**It's the only way I can get him to eat his food**

4

Why do bees have sticky hair?

**Because they have honey combs.**

▢▢▢▢

Why couldn't the bicycle stand up?

**Because it was tyred.**

**It's a world first. Five fines on the single ticket**

Knock, knock.

**Who's there?**

Alison.

**Alison who?**

Alison to my radio.

## Real life laughs

An Israeli woman who found a cockroach in her house stamped on it, threw it into the lavatory, and sprayed a full can of insecticide onto it to make sure it was dead. When her husband returned from work he threw a cigarette end into the bowl, which ignited the insecticide fumes "seriously burning his sensitive parts." Two ambulance men, shaking with laughter at the incident, dropped the stretcher he was on, sending him pitching down the stairs and breaking his pelvis and some ribs.

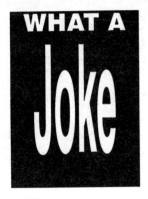

WHAT A Joke

What's green, lives in a field and has 4,000 legs?

**Grass - it was a mistake about the legs.**

• • • • • • • • • • • • • • • • • • •

Where do you take a sick horse?

**To the horsepital.**

DRACULA'S SCHOOL REPORT

**Reading:** good

**Writing:** untidy

**Cricket:** shows promise as a bat.

What's a crocodile's favourite game?

**Snap.**

What did Tarzan say when he saw the elephants come over the hill?

**Here come the elephants.**

How can you keep cool at a football match?

**Stand next to a fan.**

What do you get if you cross a crocodile with a rose?

**I don't know, but I wouldn't try smelling it.**

**As it seems like a nice weekend, I've got you some cans in...**

What is always coming but never arrives?

**Tomorrow.**

Did you hear about the two flies playing football in a saucer?

**They were practising for the cup.**

▢▢▢▢

Who did Dracula marry?

**The girl necks door.**

— ▬ ▪ ▬ ▪ ▬

**I hate spring cleaning**

Knock, knock.

**Who's there?**

Atch.

**Atch who?**

Sorry, I didn't know you had a cold.

Why did Robin Hood steal from the rich?

**Because the poor didn't have any-thing worth taking.**

**I don't know who sold you that fencing outfit, Mr Brown – but he's having you on**

**WHAT A Joke**

What's a twack?

**Something a twain runs on.**

◻◻◻◻

What animal do you look like when you have a bath?

**A little bear.**

Who was the father of the Black Prince?

**Old King Cole.**

What ring is square?

**A boxing ring.**

What do you get if you pour boiling water down a rabbit hole?

**Hot cross bunnies.**

What did the father ghost say to his son?

**Spook when you are spooken to.**

Waiter, waiter, you've got your thumb in my soup.

**That's all right, sir. It's not hot.**

What jobs do hippies do?

**They hold your leggies on.**

Doctor, doctor, I keep thinking I'm invisible.

**Who said that?**

JACK

25TH DEC

Oh heck! I've overslept!

What's yellow and white and gets eaten at 100mph?

**A train driver's egg sandwich.**

**Tell me about these hallucinations**

What did one lift say to the other lift?

**I think I'm going down with something.**

Where do policemen live?

**Letsby Avenue.**

Who gets the sack as soon as he starts work?

**A postman.**

## Real life laughs

A dead man slumped in a van parked near City Hall in Oklahoma City wasn't discovered for at least three days, even though traffic wardens had slapped 12 parking tickets on the windscreen. Leonard Hobson, 67, of Durant, had suffered a fatal heart attack

## WHAT A Joke

What was the tortoise doing on the motorway?

**About ten yards an hour.**

●●●●●●●●●●●●●●●●●●●●●●

What part of the army could a baby join?

**The infantry.**

Who's the boss of the hankies?

**The hankie chief.**

What do you feed under-nourished dwarfs?

**Elf-raising flour.**

How does a witch tell the time?

**With a witch watch.**

Why did the jockey take his hay to bed?

**To feed his nightmares.**

How do you start a pudding race?

**Sago**

What lives at the bottom of the sea with a shotgun?

**Billy the Squid.**

What exams do horses take?

**Hay levels.**

**I'd like an early evening call**

*Doctor, doctor, I've lost my memory.*

**When did it happen?**

*When did what happen?*

**He's half Dalmatian**

How do you make gold soup?

**Put nine carrots in it!**

What's a skeleton's favourite drink?

**Milk — because it's good for the bones.**

What do vampires eat for breakfast?

**Ready Nek.**

**Tom:** You wouldn't punish a student for something he didn't do, would you?

*Mrs. Smart:* No, of course not.

**Tom:** Well, I didn't do my homework.

**You Tell him**

11

**WHAT A Joke**

What did the hat say to the tie?

**You hang around while I go on ahead.**

• • • • • • • • • • • • • • • • •

What do you call two policemen?

**A pair of navy blue knickers.**

What do you get if you cross the Atlantic with the Titanic?

**Halfway.**

⬜⬜⬜⬜

Why do bees hum?

**Because they don't know the words.**

What do you get if you cross a chicken with gunpowder?

**An egg-splosion.**

⬜⬜⬜⬜

**Doctor, doctor, I think I'm a goat.**

*How long have you felt like this?*

**Since I was a kid.**

What's yellow, has twenty-two legs and goes crunch?

**A Chinese football team, eating crisps.**

Why did the bald man stick his head out of the window?

**To get some fresh hair.**

**Another restless night Mr Perkins?**

Why did the golfer have two pairs of
trousers on?

**In case he got a hole in one**.

What do you call a man
with a spade on his
head?

**Doug.**

What do you call a man
with a seagull on his
head?

**Cliff.**

□□□□

What do you call a man
without a spade on his
head?

**Dougless**

□□□□

Why did the headless
ghost go to the psychia-
trist?

**Because he wasn't all
there.**

□□□□

What happened when
Wally had a brain trans-
plant?

**The brain rejected
him.**

Breakfast in bed like you ordered!

# WHAT A Joke

Have you heard about the man who bought a paper shop?

**It blew away.**

● ● ● ● ● ● ● ● ● ● ● ●

How do hens and roosters dance?

**Chick to chick.**

Why did the farmer call his rooster Robinson?

**Because he crew so.**

Why did the chicken cross the road?

**For some fowl reason.**

What is a robbery called in Peking?

**A Chinese take-away.**

Doctor, doctor, I keep thinking I'm a dustbin.

**Don't talk rubbish.**

What's bad tempered and goes with custard?

**Apple grumble.**

Where do mummies go if they want to swim?

**The Dead Sea.**

What goes straight up in the air and wobbles?

**A jellycopter.**

**I only just made it, I can tell you**

Doctor, doctor, can you give me something for my acne?

**I never make rash promises.**

▢▢▢▢

WHAT A **Joke**

What game do horses like best?

**Stable tennis.**

What's big, red and eats rocks?

**A big red rock-eater.**

How do you make a Mexican chilli?

**Take him to the North Pole.**

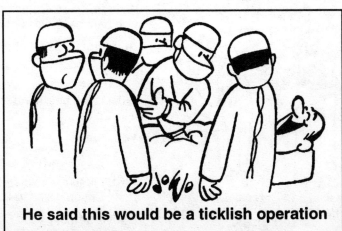

**He said this would be a ticklish operation**

15

**WHAT A JOKE**

What can you do if a herd of elephants comes racing towards you?

**Make a trunk call and reverse the charge.**

What's big and red, and lies in the gutter?

**A dead bus.**

Why does an elephant wear sneakers?

**So he can sneak up on mice.**

**Knock, knock.**
*Who's there?*
**Arfer.**
*Arfer who?*
**Arfer got.**

Why was the tomato red?

**It saw the salad dressing.**

Waiter, waiter, what are these two worms on my plate?

**Your sausages, sir.**

What do you call a gorilla with bananas in his ears?

**Anything you like - he can't hear you.**

What is the best thing to put into a pie?

**Your teeth.**

What did they do when the Forth Bridge collapsed?

**Built a fifth.**

MARRIAGE GUIDANCE

**The wife and I are slowly drifting apart – any way of speeding things up?**

16

What do you call a lady who goes into a pub and starts to juggle with the drinks?

**Beatrix.**
*(Beer tricks... geddit???)*

**Of course it's fair – you had choice of ends**

Where does Tarzan get his clothes from?

**A jungle sale.**

What do you get if you cross a centipede and a parrot.

**A walkie-talkie.**

What has four legs, an udder and flies?

**A cow.**

## Real life laughs

To combat forest fires, the French use flying boats which scoop up sea water and drop it on the blazing trees. Following one fire, searchers came upon the body of an Englishman which, according to the coroner, had fallen from a great height before being burnt. He also noted that the man was found wearing swimming trunks, a snorkel and flippers!

**WHAT A Joke**

Doctor, doctor, I think I must be invisisible. Everyone ignores me.

**Next please.**

● ● ● ● ● ● ● ● ● ● ● ● ● ● ● ●

Shall I tell you the joke about the empty house?

**There's nothing in it.**

What did the egg say in the monastery?

**Oh well, out of the frying-pan and into the friar.**

What do Eskimos call their money?

**Iced lolly.**

What happened when the carrot died?

**There was a huge turnip at the funeral.**

● ● ● ● ● ● ● ● ● ● ● ●

**Some rubbish on the box about a new advance in TV technology**

What do you get if you cross an elephant with a fish?
**Swimming trunks.**

Why are batsmen cowards?

**Because they are afraid of ducks.**

**Mum:** Why are you scratching yourself?

**Max:** Because no one else knows where I itch.

18

Why do women go to bed at night with rollers in their hair?

**So they can wake up curly in the morning**

□□□□

**Knock, knock**

*Who's there?*

**Scott**

*Scott who?*

**Scott nothing to do with you.**

What happened to the cat who swallowed a ball of wool?

**She had mittens.**

## WHAT A Joke

What do you get if you cross a stereo with a refrigerator?

**Cool music.**

● ● ● ● ● ● ● ● ● ● ● ● ● ● ● ● ●

Why did the boy throw the clock out of the window?

**To see time fly.**

What do you call a highwayman who is ill?

**Sick Turpin.**

What do you give a pony with a cold?

**Cough stirrup.**

What do you call a gorilla with a machine-gun?

**Sir!**

Did you hear about the bike that went round biting people's arms off?

**It was a vicious cycle.**

What do you get if you cross a cow, a sheep and a goat?

**A milky baaa kid!**

What do you call Postman Pat when he retires?

**Pat.**

What do cannibals eat for lunch?

**Baked beings on toast.**

Do you know the joke about chicken-pox?

**I won't tell it to you, you'd only go and pass it on.**

**Before I cure you, could you do my son's birthday party?**

Why did the chicken cross the road?

**To escape from Colonel Sanders.**

❑❑❑❑

Why are baby pigs so greedy?

**Because they want to make hogs of them-selves.**

What's white and fluffy and beats its chest in a cake shop?

**A meringue-utang.**

Why couldn't the skeleton go to the dance?

**He had no body to go with.**

Waiter, what's wrong with this fish?

**Long time, no sea, sir.**

**I wish I hadn't said my wrists were sore**

**WHAT A Joke**

**Knock knock**

*Who's there?*

**Aardvark.**

*Aardvark who?*

**Aardvark a million miles for one of your smiles.**

What did the hungry donkey say when it only had thistles to eat?

**Thistle have to do.**

● ● ● ● ● ● ● ● ● ● ● ● ● ● ● ● ● ● ● ● ●

Why can't you get milk from a mouse?

**You can't get a bucket under a mouse.**

What's the cure for water on the brain?

**A tap on the head.**

● ● ● ● ● ● ● ● ●

Waiter! There's a fly in my soup.

**That's the manager, sir. The last customer was a witch doctor.**

Did you hear about the fight in the fish shop?

**The fish got battered.**

Did you hear about the vegetarian cannibal?

**He would only eat Swedes.**

**It's either an obscene caller or Superman**

22

**Who's that at the door?**

*The Invisible Man.*

**Tell him I can't see him.**

□□□□

WHAT A Joke

**I don't want my standard of living raised.**

What goes ha ha bonk?

**A man laughing his head off.**

What do you get if you cross a skunk with a boomerang?

**A bad smell you can't get rid of.**

## Real life laughs

Assuming that the kangaroo he had shot was dead, Mr. Emilio Tarra dressed it in his Gucci blazer and was about to take its photograph when the beast recovered, knocked him out with a blow from his tail, and vanished into the bush with his passport, $2,000 and 16 credit cards.

# WHAT A Joke

**Tom :** My granny hasn't got a grey hair on her head.

**Sam:** Really?

**Tom:** Yes, she's completely bald.

● ● ● ● ● ● ● ● ● ● ● ● ● ● ● ● ● ●

What do you get if you cross an elephant with a kangaroo?

**Big holes all over Australia.**

▢▢▢▢

How does an Eskimo stop his teeth from freezing?

**He grits them.**

---

**Knock , knock.**
Who's there?
**Nick.**
Nick who?
**Nick R. Elastic.**

---

How do you make a jacket last?

**Make the trousers first.**

Why is it difficult to keep a secret at the North Pole?

**Because your teeth tend to chatter.**

What do you call an Irish spider?

**Paddy long legs.**

What coat burns?

**A blazer.**

**His last words were: my feet are killing me**

*Doctor, I think I have a split personality.*

**One patient at a time, please.**

● ● ● ● ● ● ● ● ● ● ● ● ● ● ● ● ● ● ● ● ● ● ●

**No I didn't bother to get a new licence. I only watch repeats**

What toad goes croak dot croak dot croak dot croak?

**A Morse toad.**

What happened when the bull went into the china shop?

**He had a smashing time.**

What did the traffic light say to the car?

**Don't look now, I'm changing.**

**Quick! Follow him!**

What did one pig say to the other pig?

**Will you be my pen pal.**

What kind of pudding do lawyers like best?

**Sue-t pudding.**

WHAT A Joke

What crisps fly?
**Plain ones.**

What's white and black with red spots?
**A zebra with measles.**

**Teacher:** Where are the Andes?
**Pupil:** At the end of my armies.

What do you call a bee with a quiet hum?
**A mumble bee.**

What horse can't you ride?
**A clothes horse.**

What did the baby chicken say when its mother laid an orange?
**Look what mama laid!**

● ● ● ● ● ● ● ● ● ● ● ● ● ● ● ● ● ● ●

Why couldn't the sailors play cards?
**Because the captain was standing on the deck.**

What's white and dashes through the desert with a bed pan?
**Florence of Arabia.**

What did the big candle say to the little candle?
**I'm going out tonight.**

What is the most musical fish?
**A piano tuna.**

**Nurse, fetch my binoculars**

**Doctor, doctor, I feel like a bridge.**

*What's come over you. man?*

**Well, so far two cars, three lorries and a bus.**

◻◻◻◻

**I'll bet you 10-1 you don't get away with it**

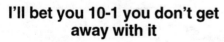

Why don't parents like their children to go near chickens?

**Because of their fowl language.**

What do you do if you find a blue banana?

**Try to cheer it up.**

What's the penalty for bigamy?

**Two mothers-in-law.**

### Real life laughts

With the full permission of a hospital in Colorado, Dr. George Balderston removed his own appendix. In the hospital's surgical theatre he sat down, anaesthetised himself, opened up his abdomen, snipped and closed the wound with clamps and stitches, unaided, within an hour.

**WHAT A Joke**

**Knock, knock,**
*Who's there?*
**Noah.**
*Noah who?*
**Noah any more knock knock jokes.**

☐☐☐☐

What's black and white
and red at the top?

**A sunburnt puffin.**

What's black and white
and red at the bottom?

**A puffin with nappy
rash.**

What's purple and flies in outer
space?

**Planet of the grapes.**

Why did the dog wear black
boots?

**His brown ones were at the
menders.**

What did the coke
say to the coal?

**What kind of fuel
am I?**

☐☐☐

What do you call a
woodpecker with no
beak?

**A headbanger.**

☐☐☐

What do you call a
snowman with a
suntan?

**A puddle.**

How do you catch a squirrel?

**Climb up a tree and act like a nut.**

Where do frogs keep their savings?

**In the river bank.**

Waiter! There's a fly in my alphabet soup!

**I expect it's learning to read , sir.**

☐☐☐

How do you make a band stand?

**Hide all their chairs.**

**Sorry about this ... but I've run out of ink**

**We've got a few ideas. Now it's just a process of elimination**

29

**WHAT A Joke**

Waiter, waiter, there's a fly in my soup.

**Don't worry , sir, that spider on your bread will get him.**

□□□□

What does the hedge-hog have for his lunch?

**Prickled onions.**

□□□

Why did the millionaire live in a mansion without a bathroom?

**Because he was filthy rich.**

Why is it cheap to feed a giraffe?

**A little goes a long way.**

How can you tell if there's an elephant in the fridge?

**There are footprints in the butter.**

● ● ● ● ● ● ● ● ● ● ● ● ● ● ● ● ● ● ● ●

Why did the blind chicken cross the road?

**To get to the birds eye shop.**

I have five noses, six mouths and seven ears. What am I?

**Very ugly.**

Doctor, doctor, I can't keep my food down. Everything I swallow comes up.

**Quick, swallow my lottery ticket.**

**What worries me is that he works for the Met Office**

**Doctor, doctor, I feel like a cricket ball.**

*How's that.*

**Don't you start.**

**Wow dad! I didn't know you could skateboard**

**Margaret:** You remind me of the sea.

**Eric:** *Why? Because I'm wild and free and romantic?*

**Margaret:** No, because you make me sick.

Why are eggs like bricks?

**They both have to be laid.**

**The sex discrimination people made me put the other one up**

**WHAT A Joke**

A man went to the doctor's. "It 's amazing, I think I can see into the future," he said.

"When did this start?" asked the doctor.

"Next week," the man replied

• • • • • • • • • • • • • • • • • • • • •

What happened to the girl who slept with her head under the pillow?

**The fairies took all her teeth away.**

Two prunes were arrested for being stewed.

**They were remanded in custardy.**

Why is a football pitch wet?

**Because the footballers dribble.**

How did the dentist become a brain surgeon?

**His drill slipped.**

🔲🔲🔲🔲

How does a witch tell the time?

**She wears a witch watch.**

Where was grandma when the lights went out?

**In the dark.**

What did the big telephone say to the little telephone?

**You're too young to be engaged.**

**I hope you're not going to grow a beard. I hate men with beards**

What's the difference between a lemon and a white elephant?

**A lemon is yellow.**

**It's all right with me, but you'd better check with the leader of the opposition**

Why did the robber take a bath?

**So he could make a clean get-away.**

Why does a witch ride on a broom?

**Because a vacuum cleaner is too heavy.**

What's bright red and very silly?

**A blood clot.**

33

# WHAT A Joke

What's white outside, grey and slimy inside, and moves very slowly.

**A slug sandwich.**

● ● ● ● ● ● ● ● ● ● ● ● ● ● ● ● ● ● ● ● ● ●

Where do baby apes sleep?

**Apricots.**

What did Adam say on the day before Christmas?

**It's Christmas Eve.**

Why is an old car like a baby?

**It never goes anywhere without a rattle.**

Where does the king keep his armies?

**Up his sleevies.**

What has a bottom at its top?

**A leg.**

Doctor, doctor, I think I'm an apple.

**Well sit down, I won't bite you.**

What kind of boats do vampires like?

**Blood vessels.**

Where does a sick ship go?

**To the dock.**

Adrian Rose

**I Henry Stimpson, being of sound mind and body ...**

Why was the patient laughing all through his operation?

**Because the doctor put him in stitches.**

REX

**This looks like the one Harry**

Why can't a man's head be twelve inches wide?

**Because if it was, it would be a foot.**

What's red and invisible?

**An invisible tomato.**

What's yellow and stupid.

**Thick custard.**

## Real life laughs

Everyone in Dartmouth, Devon, seemed to have an appropriate name in 1987. Local artist Simon Drew depicted them on a Happy Families card set. They included: Geoff Price the Bank Manager; Mike Blewitt the bookie; Charles Crisp the greengrocer; Chris Pillar the builder; Bob Crews the boatman; Derek Scorer the auction-eer; Clive Cutmore the butcher; and Dave Killer the chemist.

**WHAT A Joke**

Why do demons and ghouls get on so well together?

**Because demons are a ghouls best friend.** ✓

What's a vampire's favourite soup?

**Scream of mushroom.**

**Knock, knock.**

*Who's there?*

**Dishwasher.**

*Dishwasher who?*

**Dishwasher way I shpoke before I had falshe teeth.**

What's grey and has a trunk?

**A mouse going on holiday.**

◻◻◻◻

What did the dog say when he sat on the gravel?

**Ruff.**

Why should you never leave a box of aspirins near a bird cage?

**The parrots-eat-em-all.** ✓

Why did the little girl tiptoe past the medicine cabinet?

**She didn't want to wake the sleeping pills.**

Why did the owl howl?

**Because the woodpecker would peck 'er.**

WILDING

**I think he wants his sand-wedge**

What's big and grey and has sixteen wheels?

**An elephant on roller skates.**

◻◻◻◻

What has four wheels and flies?

**A dustcart.**

What do you call a smelly bear?

**Winnie-the-Pooh.**

What part of a fish weighs the most?

**The scales.**

**You're right. It is more full than before**

Doctor, doctor, I'm shrinking.

**You'll just have to be a little patient.**

◻◻◻

What's the difference between dentists and Christmas presents?

**Everyone loves Christmas presents.**

**Pass the cereal Madge**

WHAT A Joke

What do they call Dracula?

**A pain in the neck.**

What's bread?

**Raw toast.**

What do you get if you cross a kangaroo and a sheep.

**A woolly jumper with huge pockets.**

What did the earwig say as he fell off the wall?

**Earwig go again.**

What do you get every birthday.

**A year older.**

**Teacher:** If I had forty apples in one hand and fifty apples in the other, what would I have?

**Toby:** Big hands.

• • • • • • • • • • • • • • • • • • • • • •

CHESS TOURNAMENT

What is 600 feet high and pops up for breakfast?

**The Toast Office Tower.**

What's the definition of a cannibal?

**Someone who goes into a restaurant and orders the waiter.**

What do you get if you cross a gorilla?

**A black eye.**

Why is an elephant big, grey and wrinkly?

**Because if he was small, white and round he'd be an aspirin,**

Did you hear about the boy who had Egyptian flu?

**He caught it from his mummy.**

WHAT A Joke

**Now I know why you're always going to the pub – fun isn't it?**

What happens if you upset a cannibal?

**You get into hot water.**

Why can't leopards escape from the zoo?

**Because they're always spotted.**

What exams did Santa take at school?

**Ho-ho-ho levels.**

Doctor, doctor, I'm shrinking.

**You'll just have to be a little patient.**

What's the difference between dentists and Christmas presents?

**Everyone loves Christmas presents.**

THE END OF THE NEXT WORLD IS AT HAND

What did the knight in armour say when the king was going to give him a medal?

**You can't pin that on me, pal!**

Doctor, doctor, everyone thinks I'm a liar.

**I don't believe you.**

What's the difference between a skunk and a mouse?

**A skunk uses a cheaper deodorant.**

To what family does the rhinoceros belong?

**I don't know, but I don't think it's any in our street.**

Doctor, doctor, I feel like a snooker ball.

**Well, get to the end of the cue then.**

● ● ● ● ● ● ● ● ● ● ● ● ● ● ● ● ● ● ● ● ● ● ● ● ●

**They only open that when it's raining or snowing**

What do you get if you cross a cow with a duck?

**Cream quackers.**

❑❑❑

What did the barman say when the ghost asked for a drink?

**We don't serve spirits.**

❑❑❑

How can you get rid of a boomerang?

**Throw it down a one-way street.**

How did the carpenter regain his sight?

**He picked up his hammer and saw.**

How do you get a dinosaur to fly?

**Buy it an airline ticket.**

**The ship's doctor has been at the rum again**

**Knock, knock.**

Who's there?

**Adolf.**

Adolf who?

**Adolf ball hit me on de nose.**

What is a certain way to get a wild duck?

**Buy a tame one and annoy it.**

## Real life laughs

Lagari Hasan Celibi, pioneer of jet propulsion, made his first flight in 1633 tied to a 9-foot steel rocket, powered by gunpowder. Celibi, who undertook the task to amuse the daughter of Sultan Murad Kahn IV on her birthday, soared 900ft above the Bosphorus and landed safely in the water. According to sources "There is a strong possibility that he was drunk at the time." Following his amazing feat, Celibi was made chief rocketeer to the Turkish army.

**WHAT A Joke**

Doctor, doctor, I've eaten something that disagrees with me.

**No you haven't.**

• • • • • • • • • • • • • • • • • • • •

Waiter! There's a fly in my soup!

**Yes sir, it's the bad meat that attracts them.**

Why are flowers so lazy?

**Because they spend all day in beds.**

Why did the farmer drive a steam roller over his field?

**He wanted to grow mashed potatoes.**

What's green and hangs from trees?

**Giraffe snot.**

Officer: Okay, fire at random.

**Soldier: Yes sir. Which one is he?**

Why were the Middle Ages called The Dark Ages?

**Because there were so many knights in those days.**

When are sheep like ink?

**When they are in a pen.**

Why did the egg go into the jungle?

**Because it was an eggsplorer.**

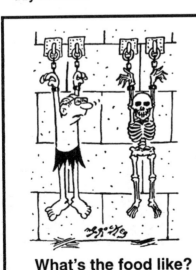

**What's the food like?**

Doctor, doctor, I've got such a headache.

**Put your head through the window and the pane will disappear.**

● ● ● ● ● ● ● ● ● ● ● ● ● ● ● ● ● ● ● ● ●

How do you make a swiss roll?

**Push him down a hill.**

How do you get rid of water on the knee?

**Wear drain-pipe trousers.**

● ● ● ● ● ● ● ● ● ● ● ● ● ●

Who said 'get stuffed' to the big bad wolf?

**Little Rude Riding Hood.**

Why do we say 'amen' not 'awomen'?

**Because we sing hymns not hers.**

**It was horrible. He got there early and Miss Muffet sat on him!**

Where do cows go on holiday?

**Moo York.**

What do you get if you are hit on the head with an axe?

**A splitting headache.**

●●●●●●●●●●●●●●●●●●●●●

Which sweet is the cleverest?

**A smartie.**

Why can't a clock see anything?

**Because it always covers its face with its hands.**

What's the result of smoking too much?

**Coffin.**

What do you call a Skoda at the top of a hill?

**A miracle.**

What's wet, black, floats on water, and shouts "knickers"?

**Crude oil.**

What's wet, black, floats on water, and shouts "Underwear"?

**Refined oil.**

What bird is always out of breath?

**A puffin.**

Two biscuits were rolling across the road. One got run over. What did the over one say?

**Crumbs.**

● ● ● ● ● ● ● ● ● ● ● ● ● ● ● ● ● ● ●

**Fred is very selective in his reading**

What animal do we get wine from?

**A wine-oceros.**

What three letters frighten robbers?

**ICU**

What do you call a bear with no hair?

**Fred bear.**

What do you get if you cross a ghost with a spider?

**A creepy crawlie.**

❑❑❑

Why is Dracula a good person to take out to dinner?

**Because he eats necks to nothing.**

**WHAT A JOKE**

Who invented the four-day week?

**Robinson Crusoe. He had all his work done by Friday.**

• • • • • • • • • • • • • • • • • • • • •

What happens if you cross a Wilton with an elephant?

**You get a huge pile on your carpet.**

What lies on the ground a hundred feet up in the air?

**A centipede lying on its back.**

*a hundred feet up in the air it lies on the ground! Tq what is it!*

What do you get if you cross a parrot with a homing pigeon?

**A bird that asks the way home.**

Why should you never tell secrets in a greengrocers?

**Because potatoes have eyes and beanstalk.**

Did you hear about the dog that ate garlic?

**His bark was worse than his bite.**

What's blue and flies through the trees?

**Tarzan in a boiler suit.**

**Dad, why are you shaving with your calculator?**

What did one eye say to the other eye?

**Between you and me something smells.**

How can you tell which end of a worm is his head?

**Tickle him in the middle and watch where he smiles.**

What do you call a deer with no eyes?

**No idea.**

What has eight legs, two humps, and flies?

**Two dead camels.**

**Need a hand with the kite dad?**

---

### Real life laughs

"Never stuff a lobster down your underpants," seems a rather obvious maxim, but one that slipped the mind of Boston shoplifter Winston Treadway. Having already secreted several items of stolen food about his person Treadway spotted a tank of live seafood in a small supermarket. He stashed a couple in his underwear and sprinted for the exit – only to stop abruptly in a nearby alley when the enraged crustaceans clamped their jaws around his genitals. Police who removed the lobsters with pliers said: "When we saw him he was trying to prise the claws off. He was purple as an egg-plant when we got to him."

## WHAT A Joke

What noise does a cat make going down the M1?

**Miaoooooooooooooooooooooow!**

● ● ● ● ● ● ● ● ● ● ● ● ● ● ● ●

What's orange and sounds like a parrot?

**A carrot.**

Doctor, doctor, I feel like a wasp.

**Buzz off.**

What's green and goes boing-boing-boing?

**A spring cabbage.**

What's black and white and noisy?

**A zebra with a set of drums.**

Why do cows wear cow bells?

**Because their horns don't work.**

Why don't gorillas like penguins?

**They can't get the wrapper off.**

What do you call a snowman in the desert?

**A wet patch in the sand.**

What's purple and burns cakes?

**Alfred the Grape.**

**It's a tough neighbourhood**

*I can make you talk like a Red Indian.*

**How?**

*See, I told you.*

▢▢▢

What goes cluck, cluck, cluck, BANG!?

**A chicken in a minefield.**

What's the nearest thing to silver?

**The Lone Ranger's bottom.**

What begins with a T, ends with a T and has T in it?

**A teapot.**

How did the Vikings send secret messages?

**By Norse code.**

How do you stop a cockerel crowing at four o'clock in the morning?

**Eat him for supper the night before.**

**I told them if I couldn't bring it with me I wouldn't come**

**WHAT A Joke**

**James:** I say, I say, I say, my cockerel's got no knees!

**Laura:** Take him to London, there are lots of Cockneys there.

• • • • • • • • • • • • • • • •

What did the frog use to cross the road?

**The green cross toad.**

---

**Knock, knock.**
Who's there?
**Nicholas.**
Nicholas who?
**Nicholas ladies shouldn't climb trees.**

---

Did you hear about the sheep dog trials?

**Three of them were guilty.**

What birds fly around in formation , very fast?

**The Red Sparrows.**

▢▢▢

What do you call a building with lots of storeys?

**A library.**

▢▢▢

What should you do if you find a gorilla in your bed?

**Sleep somewhere else.**
▢▢▢

How do you get a pat on the head?

**Sit under a cow.**

**No I'm not cross you picked it up, but we'd better take it back**

50

Why can't you starve at the seaside?

**Because of the sand which is there.**

❑❑❑

How do you make a Venetian blind?

**Poke him in the eye.**

WHAT A
Joke

**It looks like a complaint**

Why didn't the skeleton go to the disco?

**Because he had no body to dance with.**

What do you get if you cross a pet bird with a fierce dog?

**A budgerigrrrrrrrrrrrrr.**

**They say he's got money to burn – well he's met his match there**

**WHAT A Joke**

What swims in the sea, carries a machine gun, and makes you an offer you can't refuse?

**The Codfather.**

● ● ● ● ● ● ● ● ● ● ● ● ● ● ● ● ●

What do you get if you cross a fox with a chicken?

**A fox.**

How do you help a deaf fisherman?

**Give him a herring aid.**

What do you get if you cross a centipede with a parrot?

**A walkie-talkie.**

What cake gives you an electric shock?

**A currant bun.**

● ● ● ● ● ● ● ● ● ● ● ● ● ● ● ● ●

What's a frog's favourite drink?

**Croakacola.**

What race is never run?

**A swimming race.**

What did the cannibal say when he couldn't eat any more?

**I couldn't eat another mortal.**

What do policemen like best in their sandwiches?

**Truncheon meat.**

**The council says we must employ a percentage of dyslexic people**

What's yellow on the inside and green on the outside?

**A banana dressed up as a cucumber.**

□□□

Which kind of sea creature eats its victims two by two?

**Noah's shark.**

When is it unlucky to see a black cat?

**When you're a mouse.**

**It's the only way I can get him to eat his food**

**WHAT A Joke**

What did the grape say when the elephant sat on him?

**Nothing, he just gave out a little wine.**

What's black and white and red all over?

**A shy zebra.**

What sits at the bottom of the sea and shivers?

**A nervous wreck.**

How can you tell that owls are wiser than chickens?

**Have you ever seen a Kentucky Fried Owl?**

What's musical and handy in a supermarket/

**A Chopin Liszt.**

☐☐☐

What do you get if you cross a kangaroo with a hippopotamus?

**Flat Australians.**

Why did the burglar cut the legs off his bed?

**He wanted to lie low for a while.**

What do you get if you cross a ghost with a packet of crisps?

**Snacks that go crunch in the night.**

**Yes, this is Marvo the Magician speaking**

54

What is green, lives in a field and has 4,000 legs?

**Grass - I was lying about the legs.**

**Oi, just a minute**

**Woman:** I bought a carpet which was in mint condition.

**Neighbour:** What do you mean?

**Woman:** There was a hole in the middle.

□□□

What do nudists suffer from?

**Clothestrophobia.**

How do sheep keep warm at the North Pole?

**Central bleating.**

What did Santa give the octopus for Christmas?

**Four pairs of tights.**

**I paint what I see**

# WHAT A Joke

**James:** My dad wanted to stop smoking, so he tried chewing gum.

**Alex:** Did it work?

**James:** No, he couldn't get it to light.

● ● ● ● ● ● ● ● ● ● ● ● ● ● ● ● ● ●

What do you call a polar bear in a jungle?

**Lost!**

What did the Eskimo girl do to her boyfriend after an argument?

**Gave him the cold shoulder.**

What do you call a skeleton that won't get up in the morning?

**Lazy bones.**

What's big and grey, sits in a river, and squirts jam at you?

**A hippopotamus eating a dough-nut.**

What did the first mind-reader say to the second mind-reader?

**You're all right, how am I?**

What's got a head and a tail but no body?

**A coin.**

Why did the girl keep a loaf of bread in her comic?

**She liked crummy jokes.**

Why are you eating everything with your knife?

**Because my fork leaks.**

TONY
MAGICIAN

**Teacher:** If a Czar's wife is called a Czarina, what would you call her children?

**Dimwit:** Czardines?

**I'm allergic to feathers**

How did the blind carpenter regain his sight?

**He just picked up a hammer and saw.**

My wife's gone on a crash diet.

**I was wondering why she looked such a wreck.**

**Diner:** Waiter - do I have to sit here till I die of starvation?

**Waiter:** Of course not, sir. We close at eight.

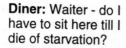

*Waiter, waiter, you've got your sleeve in my soup.*

**Don't worry, sir, there's no arm in it.**

**OK, who's the joker?**

# WHAT A Joke

Did you hear about the man who went into the pet shop and asked for a wasp? The shop assistant said they didn't sell wasps. The man said "but there is one in the window."

● ● ● ● ● ● ● ● ● ● ● ● ● ● ● ●

Doctor, doctor, can you give me something for my liver?

**How about a pound of onions and some bacon?**

▢▢▢

How does a sheep keep warm in winter?

**By central bleating.**

**Knock, knock.**

Who's there?

Juno.

**Juno who?**

Juno how long I've been waiting for you to open this door?

Why did the girl take a pencil to bed?

**To draw the curtains.**

Why did the cannibal have a bad stomach?

**Because he ate people who disagreed with him.**

Why do mother kangaroos hate wet weather?

**Because the children have to play indoors.**

Who was the skeleton who wore a kilt?

**Boney Prince Charlie.**

**Benson, I'm tired – yawn for me**

58

What do you get if you cross a skunk with a boomerang?

**A smelll that is very difficult to get rid of.**

● ● ● ● ● ● ● ● ● ● ● ● ● ● ● ● ● ● ● ●

Why did the two boa constrictors get married?

**Because they had a crush on each other.**

Doctor, doctor, I feel like a pound note.

**Go shopping, the change will do you good.**

**I think it's trying to bury its egg**

What is a beetroot?

**A potato with high blood pressure.**

What happens if you walk under a cow?

**You get a pat on the head.**

**You'd die for me? How many times?**

59

# WHAT A Joke

Why can't a car play football?

**Because it only has one boot.**

●●●●●●●●●●●●●●●●●●●●●●●

Why did the dinosaur cross the road?

**There weren't any chickens in those days.**

▢▢▢

Which musical instrument could be used for fishing?

**A cast-a-net.**

▢▢▢

Doctor, doctor, the invisible man's just outside.

**Well, tell him I can't see him without an appointment.**

What's grey, has four legs and a trunk?

**A mouse going on holiday to the sun**

What's brown, has four legs and a trunk?

**A mouse coming back off holiday.**

What do you get if you cross a snowball with a shark?

**Frostbite.**

What's the difference between frogspawn and tapioca pudding?

**Not a lot.**

Waiter, there's a hand in my soup.

**That's not your soup, sir, it's the finger bowl.**

**All right! You're only stopping the milk**

60

What did the lioness say when she found her cubs chasing a man round a tree?

**I told you not to play with your food.**

**Tarzan! Where are you?**

What do you call a cow that eats your grass?

**A lawn moo-er.**

□□□

What's the difference between a nightwatch-man and a butcher?

**One stays awake and the other weighs a steak.**

□□□

What sort of stone can you eat?

**Rock.**

□□□

**Farmer Smith:** That chicken over there is a very tough character.

**Farmer Brown:** That's because she came from a hard-boiled egg.

61

**WHAT A Joke**

What bet can never be won?

**The alphabet.**

Did you hear about the boat that sank in the sea full of piranha fish?

**It came back with a skeleton crew.**

• • • • • • • • • • • • • • • • • • • • •

Why did the thief take a bath?

**So he could make a clean getaway.**

What do you get if you cross two elephants and a fish?

**Swimming trunks.**

What do you call an Eskimo's cow?

**An Eskimoo.**

What's big and black and hairy and flies to America?

**King Kongcorde.**

**I'd like to open an account**

What kind of nut do you find in the loo?

**Peanut.**

What do you do if you find a blue banana?

**Try to cheer it up.**

Why did the punk cross the road?

**Because he was stapled to the chicken.**

**Knock, knock.**

Who's there?

**Sonia.**

Sonia who?

**Sonia foot, it's stinking the house out.**

WHAT A Joke

**Never could stand that yodelling**

How do you start a jelly race?

**Get set.**

What is a maths teacher's favourite game?

**Noughts and crosses.**

Who invented fire?

**Some bright spark.**

---

### Real life laughs

Lira banknotes worth at least £8,000 rained on Mantova, Italy in the spring of 1991. Two days later an estimated £5,000 worth fell at Frosinine, near Rome. Passers by jumped from shops and cars to excitedly gather the money and stuff it in their pockets. The wind was high on both occasions, but police had no idea where the notes came from.

**WHAT A Joke**

Why are adults always complaining?

**Because they are groan ups.**

What do you get if there is a queue outside the barber's shop?

**A barbecue.**

• • • • • • • • • • • • • • • • • • • • •

Why can't you play cards in the jungle?

**Too many cheetahs.**

How can you stop your dog from barking in the back garden?

**Put him in the front garden.**

How do you hire a horse?

**Buy it two pairs of stilts.**

What stands still and goes?

**A clock.**

How can you tell that coconut juice is nutty?

**Because it lives in a padded cell.**

*LOST PROPERTY*

**No mine didn't have any writing on**

Why did the elephant cross the road?

**Because it was the chicken's day off.**

What do you get if you cross a burglar with a bag of cement?

**A hardened criminal.**

What happened when somebody dropped a grand piano down a mine shaft?

**He got A flat minor.**

**Doctor:** Please breathe out three times.

**Patient:** Why, do you want to check my lungs?

**Doctor:** No, I want to clean my glasses.

◻◻◻

Why should you never tell pigs secrets?

**Because they're squealers.**

Did you hear about the human cannon-ball who lost his job?

**They fired him.**

◻◻◻

Mary had a little lamb, Freddie had a pup.

Johnnie had a croco-dile, which ate the others up.

◻◻◻

What do you call ghost children?

**Boys and ghouls.**

◻◻◻

**Mrs. Coakley:** What's your little boy called?

**Mrs. Knights:** Biro.

**Mrs. Coakley:** Is that his real name?

**Mrs. Knights:**

No, it's his pen name.

**You're still hitting the bar!**

**WHAT A Joke**

Why did the reindeer wear sunglasses on the beach?

**He didn't want to be recognised.**

● ● ● ● ● ● ● ● ● ● ● ● ● ● ● ● ● ● ● ● ● ● ●

Doctor, doctor, my husband thinks he's Moses.

**Tell him to stop taking the Tablets.**

How do you make anti-freeze?

**Send her to the North Pole.**

Where do chickens go to when they die?

**To the oven.**

What would you call the last rabbit in Wales?

**A Welsh Rarebit.**

How do you make an elephant die?

**Push him off the top of a sky-scraper.**

**You'd better help him with his homework now — you won't understand it soon**

Why did the chewing gum cross the road?

**Because it was stuck to the chicken's foot.**

What kind of dog hides from frying pans?

**A sausage dog.**

What would you get from a vampire that had lost its dentures?

**A very nasty suck.**

**Knock, knock.**

Who's there?
Eskimo.

**Eskimo who?**

Eskimo questions, I'll tell you no lies.

What's the difference between an elephant and a flea?

**Quite a lot, really.**

What's yellow and in a tearing hurry?

**A banana opening its birthday presents.**

How did the snowman make anti-freeze?

**He put ice-cubes in her bed**

### Free at last!

Why do African elephants have big ear?

**Because Noddy won't pay the ransom.**

What do you get if you cross a parrot and a yak?

**A yackety-yak.**

**You're late! I'm almost ready**

**WHAT A Joke**

What do you get if you cross a snake with a government employee?

**A civil serpent.**

What do you get if you cross a vampire with a mummy?

**A flying bandage.**

What's out-of-bounds at a birthday party?

**An exhausted kangaroo.**

What's wrapped in cling film and terrrorises Paris?

**The lunch-pack of Notre Dame.**

What goes cackle, cackle, bonk?

**A witch laughing her head off.**

What is the saddest thing you could get if you crossed a fruit with a vegetable?

**A melon-cauli.**

What do you call the chief sausage?

**A head banger.**

What do you get if you cross a chicken with a waiter?

**A hen that lays tables.**

What do you call an elephant that always cries when it's hit?

**A chicken.**

**Sometimes I think she understands everything we say**

Why was the chicken sitting on an axe?
**She was trying to hatchet.**

What sort of bread is stupid?
**Half-baked bread.**

What do you get if you cross the M1 with an elephant?
**Run over.**

What do you get if you cross an elephant with a hyena?
**A big laugh.**

**And the award for best actor goes to ...**

□□□

## Real life laughs

Bob Briggs, owner of Domino's Pizza in Independence, Missouri, hoped to attract business by standing outside dressed as a red rabbit. Instead, he was knocked unconscious by someone dressed as Bobo the clown, who was promoting Pizza Hut across the road.

# WHAT A Joke

What's the difference between an iceberg and a clothes brush?

**One crushes boats and the other brushes coats.**

● ● ● ● ● ● ● ● ● ● ● ● ● ●

What do you get if cross a sweet with a budgerigar?

**Fudgerigar.**

What do you call a Russian who robs lemonade factories?

**Knock your pop off.**

Why are ghosts always poor?

**Because a ghoul and his money are soon parted.**

Why do skeletons drink milk?

**Because it's good for the bones.**

Why do dragons sleep during the day?

**So they can fight knights.**

Why are racehorses like ice-creams?

**Because the more you lick them the faster they go.**

You have to take the oath. Cross my heart and hope to die is not good enough

What do you get if you cross an elephant with a pig?

**A very heavy sleeper.**

Why wasn't the elephant allowed on the aeroplane?

**His trunk was too big to fit under the seat.**

Mummy, Mummy, what's a werewolf?

**Shut up, and comb your face.**

**My horoscope says as one door closes another opens ...**

What is very large, has candles, icing and tusks?

**A mammoth birthday cake.**

**Noah:** I thought we had two turkeys when we started out.

**Mrs. Noah:** Well, dear, it is Christmas.

What's the best way to make your birthday money go a long way?

**Post it to Australia.**

What do you get if you cross a vampire with Al Capone?

**A fangster.**

**You can't complain to the manager — he has food poisoning**

# WHAT A Joke

What's 300 metres tall, weighs 7,620 tonnes and attracts bees?

**The Eiffel Flower.**

● ● ● ● ● ● ● ● ● ● ● ● ● ● ● ● ● ● ● ● ● ●

What kind of food is cheeky?

**Food with a lot of sauce.**

How does Batman's mother call him in for his supper?

**Dinner, dinner, dinner, dinner, Batman.**

Why should you tiptoe past the chemist?

**So you don't wake the sleeping pills.**

What do you call a dog with a bunch of daisies on its head?

**A collie-flower.**

What weights four tons, is grey and loves curry?

**An Indian elephant.**

How does an elephant overtake a tortoise?

**He steps on it.**

Where would you buy a birthday present for Superman?

**At a supermarket.**

**You're pulling the stiches too tight Smedley!**

What did the dog say to the reindeer?

**Woof, woof.**

What is small, has pointed ears and is a great detective?

**Sherlock Gnomes.**

What do you call a tug-of-war on 24th December?

**Christmas Heave.**

What sort of chocolates live at the bottom of the sea?

**Oyster eggs.**

**Watch out for his footwork**

What happened to the chicken that had a hot bath?

**It laid hard-boiled eggs.**

❑❑❑

Did you hear about the wizard who went out with the twin witches?

**It was very confusing because he couldn't tell which witch was witch.**

**Who are you talking to Harry?**

**WHAT A Joke**

How can you tell when an elephant has cut its toenails?

**The scissors are blunt.**

● ● ● ● ● ● ● ● ● ● ● ● ● ● ● ● ● ● ● ● ● ●

What's white and goes up?

**A silly snowflake.**

**Knock, knock.**
Who's there?
**Lettuce.**
Lettuce who?
**Lettuce in quickly, it's raining.**

Why didn't the skeleton want to go to school?

**Because his heart wasn't in it.**

When was the Iron Age?

**Before drip-dry shirts were invented.**

How do the Welsh eat cheese?

**Very Caerphilly.**

What do you call an elephant listening in to a conversation?

**Big ears.**

Why do all elephants have grey trunks?

**They all belong to the same swimming club.**

**How would you like to do a spot of modelling? They want a new pub sign at the Nag's Head.**

What's yellow on the inside and pink with candles on the outside?

**A banana disguised as a birthday cake.**

● ● ● ● ● ● ● ● ● ● ● ●

**Of course it isn't serious — now hurry up and take your medicine**

Where should the twenty-pound banana go?

**On a diet.**

What do you think the tiniest vampire in the world gets up to at night?

**Your ankles.**

Did you hear about the stupid turkey?

**He was looking forward to Christmas.**

What is Dracula's motto?

**The morgue the merrier.**

What do you call a dinosaur who can't walk properly?

**A Staggersaurus.**

## WHAT A Joke

What happened to the nut that was beaten up?

**It was an assaulted peanut.**

□□□

What happened to the elephant when he drank too much?

**He got trunk.**

• • • • • • • • • • • • • • • • • • • •

Did you hear about the new vampire doll?

**You wind it up and it bites Barbie on the neck.**

What are baby witches called?

**Halloweenies.**

• • • • • • • • • • • • • • • •

What do you call a very nervous witch?

**A twitch.**

How can you make a witch itch?

**Take away her W.**

Why did the man have a sausage stuck behind his ear?

**Because he'd just eaten his pencil.**

What did Mrs Christmas say to her husband during the storm?

**Come and look at the reindeer.**

What's green and goes boing-boing-boing?

**Spring cabbage.**

**Normal service will be resumed as soon as you've paid your rental**

What are wedge-shaped aspirins for?

**For splitting headaches.**

What would you call a badly behave potato that watches football?

**A common-tater.**

What do you get if you cross an elephant with a crow?

**Lots of broken telegraph poles.**

Where would a cannibal go for a snack?

**Anywhere they served people.**

What is an Ig?

**An Eskimo's house without a loo.**

**We'll miss you.
It was nice having neighbours we didn't have to keep up with**

77

# WHAT A Joke

Knock, knock.

Who's there?

**Irish Stew.**

Irish Stew who?

**Irish stew in the name of the law.**

What sits in a pushchair and wobbles?

**A jelly baby.**

❑❑❑

What is grey and powdery?

**Instant elephant.**

Why should you wear a tartan waistcoat?

**To keep your tummy in check.**

❑❑❑

What did the burglar get when he stole a calendar?

**Twelve months.**

**It's not a bad round, apart from this one house**

If all the cars in Britain were pink, what would you have?

**A pink car nation.**

Why did the witch put her broom in the washing-machine?

**She wanted a clean sweep.**

What do you call an Irish flying insect?

**Paddy Long-legs.**

**Doctor, doctor, for the last ten years my sister has believed she is a hen?**

Goodness gracious, why didn't you come to me sooner?

**We needed the eggs.**

Why was the crab arrested?

**Because he kept pinching things.**

What do misers do in cold weather?

**Sit round a candle.**

*sits* ✓

What do misers do in very cold weather?

Light it.

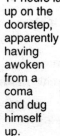

---

### Real life laughs

Glen Maloney's Jack Russell terrier, Mugsy was hit by a car in Maryland, USA. Glen thought the dog was dead and buried it in a three foot grave while his children cried indoors. 14 hours later, Mugsy turned up on the doorstep, apparently having awoken from a coma and dug himself up.

**WHAT A Joke**

Excuse me, did you know that you have jelly in one ear and custard in the other?

**I'm sorry, you'll have to speak louder, I'm a trifle deaf.**

What do you call a cat that eats lemons?

**Sourpuss.**

What's the most important thing you can take into the desert?

**A thirst-aid kit.**

What do you call a witch who goes to the beach but won't go into the water?

**A chicken sandwitch.**

Why is the Yorkshire cricket team like a Yorkshire pudding?

**Because they both rely on good batters.**

What's the difference between a toothbrush and an elephant?

**You can't clean your teeth with an elephant.**

What game do cows like playing?

**Moo-sical chairs.**

Why does Father Christmas like to work in the garden?

**Because he likes to hoe, hoe, hoe.**

**I thought the tickets were very cheap for a dinner dance!**

Where do ghosts go at Christmas?

**To a phantomime.**

❑❑❑

What is bright red and dumb?

**A blood clot.**

What happened when the wheel was invented?

**It caused a revolution.**

❑❑❑

What do you get if you cross an elephant with a computer?

**A ten-ton know it all.**

❑❑❑

How did seven hippos fit under one umbrella and not get wet?

**It wasn't raining.**

❑❑❑

Why do bees fly with their legs crossed?

**Because they are looking for B.P. stations.**

❑❑❑

Which food gets scared easily?

**Chicken pie.**

**WHAT A Joke**

What do vampires take for a bad cold?

**Coffin drops.**

▢▢▢

How do you phone the sun?

**Use a sundial.**

• • • • • • • • • • • • • • • • • • • • •

What do you call a train full of sweets?

**A chew chew.**

Did you hear about the potato that went continental?

**It became a French fry.**

What do you get if you cross an elephant with a skunk?

**A big stinker.**

What do tight-rope walkers eat?

**Anything, so long as it's a balanced meal.**

What kind of plate does a skeleton eat off?

**Bone china.**

What do you call a skeleton that never does any work?

**Lazy bones.**

What do Liverpool football fans sing at Christmas?

**Yule never walk alone....**

How does a snowman travel around?

**By icicle.**

**Ever had one of those days when you just can't seem to do anything right?**

What do you get if you cross an elephant with a watchdog?

**Very nervous postmen.**

❏❏❏

What goes in grey and comes out blue?

**An elephant swimming on a cold day.**

**He's a very efficient guard dog**

As shepherds watched their flocks by night,

All tuned to BBC,

The angel of the Lord came down,

And switched to ITV.

**Doctor, doctor, I think I'm an apple.**

*Don't worry, I won't bite you.*

Why are fish easy to weigh?

**Because they've got their own scales.**

What's green and noisy?

**A froghorn.**

What are baby soldiers called?

**Infantry.**

She was a good housekeeper-she got the house!

# WHAT A Joke

**Father cannibal to daughter:** It's time you got married. We'll start looking for an edible bachelor.

What's the difference between a train driver and a teacher?

**One minds the train and the other trains the mind.**

• • • • • • • • • • • • • • • • • • • • • • •

What has icing and candles and hums?

**A birthday cake that doesn't know the words.**

What did the stamp say to the envelope?

**Stick with me and we'll go places.**

How do you get down from an elephant?

**You don't, you get down from a duck.**

What do you call a man with a car on his head?

**Jack.**

Why are Dracula's teeth like stars?

**Because they come out at night.**

Why did Henry VIII have so many wives?

**Because he liked to chop and change.**

How do you help a drowning mouse?

**Give it mouse to mouse resuscitation.**

**I don't like the shape. Could you make it sort of pointed?**

**Knock, knock.**

Who's there?

**Micky.**

Micky who?

**Micky won't fit, that's why I'm knocking.**

How do you get an elephant into a car?

**Open the door.**

□□□

How did the monkey make toast?

**He put it under a gorilla.**

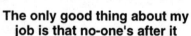

**The only good thing about my job is that no-one's after it**

Waiter! This chick is very oily.

**Yes, sir, it's a slick chick.**

What lives in Scotland and never wins the football pools?

**The Luckless Monster.**

# WHAT A Joke

How do you get a paper baby?

**Marry an old bag.**

□□□

When is a car not a car?

**When it's turned into a lay-by.**

• • • • • • • • • • • • • • • • • • • • • • • •

What reptiles are good at arithmetic?

**Adders.**

Why did the cannibal feel sick after eating the missionary?

**Because you can't keep a good man down.**

What do you get if you cross a pig with the M1?

**A road hog.**

What do you call a fish with no eyes?

**Fsh.**

Who was the fastest runner?

**Adam. He was first in the human race.**

What do you get if you cross a teddy bear with a pig?

**A teddy boar.**

Doctor, doctor, I keep thinking there's two of me.

**One at a time, please.**

What's big, red, and lies upside down in the gutter?

**A dead bus.**

Lesley Anne

**Can't come to play - I've got to help dad with my homework**

What was the cannibal called who ate his father's sister?

**An aunt-eater.**

What's green and holds up stage-coaches?

**Dick Gherkin.**

How did the Paris police find Quasimodo?

**They followed a hunch.**

Why are skeletons usually so calm?

**Nothing gets under their skin.**

**Don't worry about your job - it's been advertised and no-one wants it!**

## Real life laughs

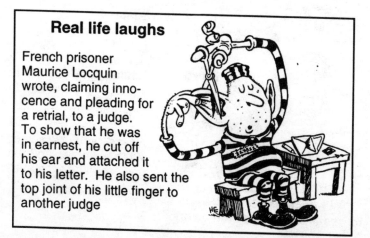

French prisoner Maurice Locquin wrote, claiming innocence and pleading for a retrial, to a judge. To show that he was in earnest, he cut off his ear and attached it to his letter. He also sent the top joint of his little finger to another judge

**WHAT A Joke**

What happens if you put a bell on the kitchen scales?

**You get jingles all the weigh.**

How can you stop an elephant from smelling?

**Tie a knot in its trunk.**

• • • • • • • • • • • • • • • • • • • • •

Why do monkeys never forget birthdays?

**They like dates.**

What's white and fluffy and always comes back when you throw it?

**Boomeringue.**

How do you stop a dog digging holes in your garden?

**Hide his spade.**

Why did the cat run away when you shouted at her?

**You hurt her felines.**

If I were you, I'd snap it up before it goes

What cheese is made backwards?

**Edam.**

How do you make a slow reindeer fast?

**Don't feed it.**

What do you give someone who has everything?

**Penicillin.**

Why did Dracula like to help young vampires?

**Because he liked to get some new blood in the business.**

What monkey looks like a flower

**A chimp-pansy.**

**Can't make it out.
According to this, it's midday!**

Who is the meanest person in the world?

**A man who finds a sling and then breaks his arm to wear it.**

What's the best system of book keeping?

**Never lend them.**

How do you get a baby to go to sleep on the moon?

**Rocket.**

**Better get home. I popped out for a quick pint while the wife cooks the Christmas dinner...**

# WHAT A Joke

*Doctor, doctor, I keep thinking I'm a dog.*

*Lie down on this couch and I'll examine you.*

*I can't. I'm not allowed on the furniture.*

● ● ● ● ● ● ● ● ● ● ● ● ● ● ● ● ● ● ●

Waiter, waiter, this coffee tastes like mud.

**I'm not surprised, madam. It was only ground a moment ago.**

Where do elves go to get fit?

**Elf farms.**

Have you heard about the two men who opened up a restaurant on the moon?

**The food was good, but the place lacked atmosphere.**

▢▢▢

What's round, white and giggles?

**A tickled onion.**

What invention enables you to see through the thickest walls?

**The window.**

▢▢▢

How long does a candle take to burn down?

**About one wick.**

▢▢▢

What do you have to take to become a coroner?

**A stiff exam.**

▢▢▢

Why is a river lazy?

**Because it seldom gets out of its bed.**

**You're right, I am on time - my watch must be wrong!**

What were the gangster's last words?

**Who put that violin in my case?**

What's black and white and goes round and round?

**A puffin in a revolving door.**

How can you tell if there's an elephant in the refrigerator?

**You can't shut the door.**

☐☐☐

**First cannibal:** We had burglars last week.

**Second cannibal:** Did they taste good?

**Knock Knock**

Who's there?

**Wendy.**

Wendy who?

**Wendy heck are you going to let me in.**

☐☐☐

Why does lightning shock people?

**It doesn't know how to conduct itself.**

**Does this mean I failed my driving test?**

## WHAT A Joke

What do you call a neurotic octopus?

**A crazy, mixed-up squid.**

What do you call a girl who lies across the middle of a tennis court?

**Annette.**

• • • • • • • • • • • • • • • • • • • • • • •

What do you call a man with a rabbit up his jumper?

**Warren.**

What do you call a girl who stands with one leg on each side of a river?

**Bridget.**

What bird spends most of its time on its knees?

**A bird of prey.**

What gets wetter as it dries?

**A towel.**

• • • • • • • • • • •

What wears a coat all winter and pants all summer?

**A dog.**

▢▢▢

What sort of cake do you not want on your birthday?

**Stomach-ache.**

▢▢▢

What's grey, weighs four tons and lives in California?

**An L.A. Phant.**

▢▢▢

What is the definition of a doughnut?

**A crazy millionaire.**

**You've never really liked that cat, have you?**

What did the electrician's wife say when he arrived home late?

**Wire you insulate?**

ㅁㅁㅁ

What did the bell say when it fell in the water?

**I'm wringing wet.**

**The brakes don't work but it's OK - the horn is very loud...**

How do you know a sausage doesn't like being fried?

**Because it spits.**

Did you hear about the plastic surgeon?

**He sat in front of the fire and melted**

Doctor, doctor, I keep stealing things.

**Try these pills. And if they don't work, bring me back a compact disc player.**

ㅁㅁㅁ

*Granddad, do you know how to croak?*

I don't think so, Stanley, why?

*Because Dad says he'll be rich when you do.*

He leaves the lawn the same way he leaves the pub - half cut

**WHAT A Joke**

**Knock, knock.**
Who's there?
**Bernadette.**
Bernadette who?
**Bernadette my dinner.**

How do you cure acid indigestion.

**Don't drink acid.**

How did the boy and girl vampire fall in love?

**At first fright.**

What happens if a frog's car breaks down?

**It gets toad away.**

What do you call a man who gets up your nose?

**Vic.**

What do angry rodents send at Christmas?

**Cross-mouse cards.**

How can you tell when an elephant is in the school custard?

**When it is more lumpy than usual.**

What fish swims at a hundred miles an hour?

**A motorpike.**

**I'm sorry Mr Smith – there's not much call for bird impersonators**

What did the bee say to the flower?

**Hello, honey.**

94

What do you give a seasick gorilla?

**Plenty of room.**

What do you call a sheep with a machine-gun?

**Lambo.**

WHAT A Joke

**Teacher:** Where do you find giant snails?

**Girl:** On a giant's fingers and toes.

Why was the teacher cross-eyed?

**He couldn't control his pupils.**

Why did the tortoise cross the road?

**To get to the Shell Garage.**

What goes 'quick, quick'?

**A duck with hiccups.**

Which is the fastest, heat or cold?

**Heat, because you can catch a cold.**

**Stop mucking about – just bring my slippers**

Did you hear about the stupid ghost?

**He climbed over walls.**

*Doctor, doctor, I think I'm allergic to liquorice.*

**Well, it takes Allsorts to make a world.**

What do you call the spot in the middle of a graveyard?

**The dead centre.**

Why do skeletons hate the winter?

**Because the cold goes straight through them.**

What do witches like best for lunch?

**Toad-in-the-hole.**

What do you call a hairy beast that's lost?

**A where-wolf.**

• • • • • • • • • • • • • • • • • • • •

What happens when the Queen burps?

**She issues a royal pardon.**

❑❑❑

What do cars do at discos?

**A brake dance.**

❑❑❑

What's the difference between a sailor and a bargain shopper?

**One goes to sail the seas, the other to see the sales.**

Did you hear about the wally who insisted on buying a black and white dog?

**He thought the licence was cheaper.**

**It's a new BBC campaign to combat licence dodgers**

What goes 'gobble, gobble, bang'?

**A turkey in a minefield.**

What do you get if you cross an Egyptian mummy with a swot?

**Someone who is wrapped up in his work.**

She stood on the bridge at midnight,

Her lips were all a-quiver.

She gave a cough, her leg fell off,

And floated down the river.

What do you call a cat who has swallowed a duck?

**A duck-filled-fatty-puss.**

**How's the baby? We thought you'd never ask**

## WHAT A Joke

Why did the baker get an electric shock?

**He stood on a bun and the currant ran up his leg.**

• • • • • • • • • • • • • • • • • • • • • • •

What lives in the sea and pulls teeth?

**The dental sturgeon.**

What is the most untidy part of a ship?

**The officers' mess.**

What do you call a Scottish chef?

**Dinner Ken.**

What's blue and has big ears?

**An elephant at the North Pole.**

What do you get if an elephant sits on your best friend?

**A flat mate.**

What is the favourite pasta dish in America?

**Yankee Noodles.**

What is full of sandwiches and calls out, 'The bells, the bells'

**The Lunchpack of Notre Dame.**

Why didn't anyone recognise the biscuit?

**Because it had been a wafer too long.**

**Are you sure you're doing an acupuncture course?**

Mary had a little lamb
It was her birthday treat.
She wolfed the lot in half-an-hour
Then wanted more to eat.

What do you give a hippo on board ship?

**A wide berth.**

Why did the robber take a bath?

**So he could make a clean get-away**

## Real life laughs

*Nothing, Arizona, a desert service stop community off Route 93 with a population of four, was hit by fire on 5 July 1988 and reduced to really noth-ing.*

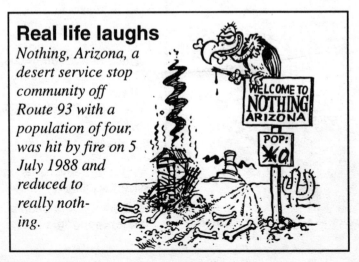

**WHAT A Joke**

**Knock, knock.**
Who's there?
**Cornflakes.**
Cornflakes who?
**I'll tell you next week, it's a cereal.**

• • • • • • • • • • • • • • • • • • • • •

How do you wish a fish 'Happy Birthday'?

**Drop him a line.**

What's the difference between a biscuit and a reindeer?

**You can't dunk a reindeer in your tea.**

Why did the secretary have the ends of her fingers amputated?

**So she could write shorthand.**

Waiter, what's this fly doing in my soup?

**Breaststroke, sir!**

What's mad and goes to the moon?

**A loony module.**

How did the dinosaurs know we were coming?

**Because the Bronto-saw-us.**

Why is a radio never complete?

**It's always a wireless.**

Why does Dracula live in a coffin?

**Because the rent is low.**

**Looks like someone's come to view the house, dear...**

100

What do you get if you cross mouldy peas with rotten eggs, soggy cabbage, potato peel and grease?

**School dinners.**

**WHAT A Joke**

Where does Dracula get all his jokes?

**From his cryptwriter.**

□□□

Who said 'shiver me timbers' on the ghost ship?

**The skeleton crew.**

□□□

What is big and grey and plays squash?

**An elephant in a cupboard.**

□□□

Why are cooks bullies?

**They whip the cream and beat the eggs.**

□□□

Why did the cleaning woman stop cleaning?

**Because she found grime doesn't pay.**

**Everyone's equal here - you'll be paid as little as the rest of them**

# WHAT A Joke

The boy stood on the burning deck
His feet were full of blisters
The flames came up and burned his pants
So now he wears his sister's

• • • • • • • • • • • • • • • • • • • • • •

**What do cannibals play at birthday parties?**

**Swallow my leader.**

Did you hear about the man who stole some rhubarb?

**He was put into custardy.**

What kind of monster can sit on the end of your finger?

**A bogeyman.**

What kind of salad speaks for itself?

**A tongue salad.**

When do you get that run-down feeling?

**When you've been hit by a car.**

What's black and white, and goes moo, moo, splat?

**A cow falling over a cliff.**

What do you call a woman who doesn't like butter?

**Marge.**

When is a door not a door?

**When it's ajar.**

**He wanted a cowboy outfit – builders' overalls and toolbox**

I eat my peas with honey;
I've done it all my life.
It makes the peas taste funny,
But it keeps them on the knife.

What's worse than finding a maggot in your apple?

**Finding half a maggot.**

☐☐☐

What goes chuff-chuff at a wedding?

**The bride's train.**

☐☐☐

What do you get if you cross a cow, a sheep and a goat?

**A milky-baa kid.**

**What, even the maths teacher?**

Hickory dickory dock

**Three mice ran up the clock**

**The clock struck one ...**

**and the other two got away with minor injuries.**

# WHAT A Joke

What grows in gardens, makes a sandwich and is dangerous if you run into it?

**A hambush.**

• • • • • • • • • • • • • • • • • • • • •

What weighs two thousand pounds and wears a flower behind its ear?

**A hippy potamus.**

What's green and slimy and goes hith?

**A snake with a lisp.**

What runs around forests making other animals yawn?

**A wild bore.**

What can fall on water without getting wet?

**A shadow.**

What sits in a fruit bowl and shouts for help?

**A damson in distress.**

What are two rows of cabbages called?

**A dual cabbage-way.**

What race is never run?

**A swimming race.**

When is a red-headed idiot like a biscuit?

**When he's a ginger nut.**

Why is the theatre such a sad place?

**The seats are always in tiers.**

Why is pork like an old radio?

**Because they both have a lot of crackling.**

What do you call a clever biscuit?

**A smart cookie.**

**Being my own boss is OK - but the staff dance is a washout**

Why don't elephants eat penguins?

**They can't get the wrappers off.**

How do ghosts like their eggs?

**Terror-fried.**

Why is the letter E lazy?

**Because it's always in bed.**

Where do all good turkeys go when they die?

**To oven.**

Have you heard about the man who drove his car over a cliff?

**He wanted to test the air brakes.**

Nothing new about neighbourhood watch. My wife's an expert...

# WHAT A Joke

Why did the turkey cross the road?

**To prove that he wasn't a chicken.**

What's got a long neck, is big and grey?

**A giraffe disguised as an elephant.**

• • • • • • • • • • • • • • • • • • • • •

What are assets?

**Little donkeys.**

Why did the policeman cry?

**Because he couldn't take his panda to bed.**

What grows up while it grows down?

**A baby duckling.**

• • • • • • • • • • • • • • • • • •

Where were chips first fried?

**In Greece.**

What type of dog goes into a corner every time a bell rings?

**A boxer.**

What do you get if you give a chicken whisky?

**Scotch eggs.**

What kind of bird do you find down a coal-pit?

**A mynah bird.**

What language do twins speak in Holland?

**Double Dutch.**

**Please call a plumber Fred - we can't afford to let you repair it**

**Customer:** I'd like a mousetrap, please.

*Chemist:* Have you tried Boots?

**Customer:** I'd like to catch it, not kick it to death.

WHAT A Joke

**If my violin lessons annoy you, feel free to complain to my mother...**

Why does a dog chase its tail?

**To make both ends meet.**

Which of the United States is round at the ends and high in the middle?

**Ohio.**

**Real life laughs**
Andrew Giles, from Wakefield, West Yorkshire, attempted to rob a shop by using a courgette as an imitation firearm.

## WHAT A Joke

What does an executioner do with a notepad and a pencil?

**Writes his chopping list.**

There's a man at the door with a drum.

**Tell him to beat it.**

● ● ● ● ● ● ● ● ● ● ● ● ● ● ● ● ● ● ● ●

When earwigs go to a football match they all chant "Earwigo-ear-wigo-earwigo.

*Teacher:* Name four animals of the cat family.

**Boy:** Father cat, mother cat, and two kittens.

---

Forth from his den to steal he stole.

His bags of chink he chunk.

And many a wicked smile he smole,

And many a wink he wunk.

---

What's the difference between a wet day and a boy at the dentist's?

**One pours with rain, the other roars with pain.**

**Man:** Do you like being a chimney sweep?

**Sweep:** Yes, it soots me.

What song did Cinderella sing when she took her holiday films to the chemist's?

**Some day my prints will come....**

**Forget it brother Giles - the milkman's been and gone**

A man goes into Casualty with an injured arm. The doctor examines him and says he's broken it. The man asks,

"Will I be able to play the piano?"

"Yes" replies the doctor.

"That's funny", says the man, "I couldn't play it before".

● ● ● ● ● ● ● ● ● ● ● ● ● ● ● ● ● ● ● ● ●

WHAT A Joke

What did the elephant say to the alligator when it bit his trunk off?

**I subbose you fink dat's funny.**
☐☐☐

Why is getting up at three o'clock in the morning like a pig's tail?

**It's twirly.**

## You've never mad a rock garden before, have you?

What did one pencil say to the other?

**I've got a terrible leadache.**
☐☐☐

What's the difference between a fisherman and a bad boy at school?

**One baits his hooks and the other hates his**

Yes, daddy's got a pink shirt, and spotted under- pants - why?

# WHAT A Joke

What do you call it when a ghost makes a mistake?

**A boo-boo.**

❑❑❑

What trees do ghosts like best?

**Ceme-trees.**

• • • • • • • • • • • • • • • • • • • •

What do you call a vampire that lies on the floor all the time?

**Matt.**

Which town in Britain makes the unhealthiest sandwiches?

**Oldham.**

What's purple and close to France?

**Grape Britain.**

❑❑❑

What do you get if you cross a vampire with a mummy?

**A flying bandage.**

Why did the sailor grab a cake of soap when his ship was sinking?

**He hoped he would be washed ashore.**

❑❑❑

What do you get if you cross a dog with a four wheel drive vehicle?

**A Land-Rover.**

❑❑❑

What did Mrs. Spider say when Mr. Spider broke her new web?

**Darn it.**

We didn't plan a pool. Fred started changing a tap washer and things got a bit out of control...

110

What did the dog say to the bone?

**It's nice gnawing you.**

What happened to the naughty egg?

**It was eggspelled from school.**

**I come from a broken home - I've just broken it**

Waiter, there's a fly in my soup.

*Would you like it zipped up, sir?*

□□□

**Waiter, there's a dead fly in my soup.**

*Yes, sir, it's the heat that kills them.*

What wobbles by remote control?

**Jelly vision.**

□□□

Why wouldn't the peach marry the banana?

**Because it had a heart of stone.**

□□□

What's the definition of illegal?

**A sick bird.**

**You mean while we've been trying to keep up with you, you've been trying to keep up with us?!**

**WHAT A Joke**

Which Italian artist wobbled?

**Botti Jelly.**

What is white, furry and smells of peppermint?

**A polo bear.**

• • • • • • • • • • • • • • • • • • • • • • •

Why did the turtle cross the road?

**Because the chicken was on holiday.**
☐☐☐

What's the difference between a penguin and an elephant?

**You can eat a p- p-p-Penguin.**

What kind of dog do you find in a vegetable plot?

**A Jack Brussel.**
☐☐☐

Where do sick horses go?

**To the Horspital.**
☐☐☐

Where do sheep have their hair cut?

**At the baabaa's.**

Where do tadpoles change into frogs?

**In the croak-room.**
☐☐☐

Doctor, doctor, I feel like a bee.

**Well, give me a buzz if things get worse.**
☐☐☐

Why aren't 15 year olds allowed to vote?

**East 17 would be the next Prime Minister.**

**Working late at the office? But you mix cement on a building site!**

112

What do you do if you see a spaceman?

**Park in it, man.**

□□□

What goes out brown and comes back white?

**A teddy bear in a snow storm.**

**If you do well, Mrs Jones, I'll get in the car with you next week**

● ● ● ● ● ● ● ● ● ● ● ● ● ● ● ● ●

Why are elephants so wrinkled?

**Have you ever tried ironing one.**

□□□

Why did the prune go out with a sultana?

**Because he couldn't find a date.**

What do you do with a rubber trumpet?

**Join an elastic band.**

□□□

Why did you call your dog Coffee?

**Because he keeps us awake all night.**

**...and it's conveniently near the railway station**

113

**WHAT A Joke**

Why couldn't the butterfly go to the dance?

**It was a moth ball.**

❑❑❑

What dance can you do in the bathroom?

**A tap dance.**

● ● ● ● ● ● ● ● ● ● ● ● ● ● ● ● ● ●

What did one curtain say to the other curtain?

**Well, I'll be hanged.**

❑❑❑

My granny has teeth like stars.

*Really?*

Yes - they come out at night.

What do you call a very small mother?

**Minimum .**

❑❑❑

What's a prickly pear?

**Two hedgehogs.**

❑❑❑

Why is it easy to fool a shark?

**They'll swallow anything.**

What's black and shiny, off its rocker, and lives at the Tower of London?

**A raven loony.**

❑❑❑

What do you call a train full of toffee?

**A chew chew train.**

❑❑❑

What do you call an underground train full of professors?

**A tube of smarties.**

**It isn't serious. It just needs a rest!**

Her death it brought us bitter woe,
Yea, to the heart it wrung us.
And all because she didn't know
A mushroom from a fungus.

Why are ghosts bad at telling lies?

**Because you can see right through them.**

◻◻◻

Why did the two cyclops fight?

**They could never see eye to eye over anything.**

When is steak very expensive?

**When it's rare.**

◻◻◻

What food is good for the brain?

**Noodle soup.**

◻◻◻

How do turkeys communicate?

**They use fowl language.**

**Your husband phoned, complaining about a blurred picture**

**WHAT A Joke**

What do ghosts in hospital talk about?

**Their apparitions.**

Did you hear about the Chinese waiter who was depressed?

**He committed chop sueycide.**

What did one worm in the graveyard say to the other?

**I have something to tell you in dead Ernest.**

What happened to Ray when he fell off the cliff?

**He became an X-Ray.**

How do you calculate the colour of plums?

**Use a green gauge.**

Why is the apple-tree crying?

**Because people are always picking at him.**

**Our neighbourhood watch sign? Someone stole it...**

What do Prince Charles and an elephant have in common?

**Nothing.**

What is the best way to catch an elephant?

**Act like a nut and he'll follow you anywhere.**

What's big, wrinkled and green?

**An unripe elephant.**

Where do you get a birthday present for your dog?

**British Bone Stores.**

Why is a banana-skin like a pullover?

**Because it's easy to slip on.**

Why did the jelly wobble?

**Because it saw the milk shake.**

This'll teach next door to boast about their Doberman...

# WHAT A Joke

Waiter, waiter, this egg tastes off.

**Don't blame me, sir. I only laid the table.**

What do a dog and a tree have in common?

**Bark.**

• • • • • • • • • • • • • • • • • • •

When is a black dog not a black dog?

**When it's a greyhound.**

Why was the dog called Johann Sebastian?

**Because of his Bach.**

Why did the cat join the Red Cross?

**Because he wanted to be a first aid kit.**

Where do ghost trains stop?

**At a manifestation.**

• • • • • • • • • • • • • • • • •

When is a dog like a camera?

**When it snaps.**

Which part of a cake does the dentist make?

**The filling.**

What biscuits do idiots like?

**Crackers.**

**To make things simpler I filed them all under 'Dear Sir'**

A ghost went to the pub and ordered a glass of whiskey. " I'm sorry, said the landlord, "but we don't have a licence to serve spirits".

WHAT A Joke

**Yum-yum, rats today.  Make mine medium rare - he has crispy roast**

**James:** My sister got underwater grades in all her GCSEs.

**Sam:** Underwater grades?

**James:** Yes - below C level.

As shepherds washed their socks by night,

All seated round the tub,

A bar of Sunlight soap came down,

And they began to scrub.

**I have to leave it in an enormous car park**

# WHAT A Joke

Burglars have stolen all the lavatories from the police station. Detective Kipper told reporters, "So far we have nothing to go on".

What happens if you eat uranium?

**You'll get atomic ache.**

❑❑❑

*Doctor, doctor, I feel like a window.*

**Do you have a pain?**

❑❑❑

Did you hear about the doctor who had to give up his job?

**He simply didn't have the patients for it.**

What happened to the burglar who fell into a pile of cement?

**He became a hardened criminal.**

What's the definition of a criminal?

**Someone who gets caught.**

• • • • • • • • • • • • • • • • • • • • •

What happened when the witch swallowed a frog?

**She croaked.**

What kind of shoes do witches wear in the summer?

**Open-toad sandals.**

What do you call a thief who breaks into a fast food restaurant?

**A hamburglar.**

**We're one big happy family here - unfortunately you're leaving home**

What goes dot dot ribbet ribbet dash dash

**Morse toad.**

What's yellow and stupid?

**Thick custard.**

□□□

What's pink, wobbly and flies?

**A jellycopter.**

**You see, there is enough room!**

## WHAT A Joke

What do you call a thin mouse?

**A narrow squeak.**

**They built a bungalow - then found they had some bricks over...**

**This is a selection from the best of Crime Watch**

Which birds are religious?

**Birds of prey.**

◻◻◻

What did one hippie ghost say to the other hippie ghost?

**Real ghoul, man.**

◻◻◻

What ship would you take to a party?

**An ice-breaker.**

What do you call a sleeping bull?

**A bull-dozer.**

□□□

**Don't invite them again - we can never get rid of them**

When is the best time to buy a canary?

**When it's going cheap.**

## Real life laughs

At the age of 30, Adam Newman, now 58, of Sydney, Australia heard "the spirit" telling him to build an ark before the great rains. He has three floating arks but is in trouble with the local government because he is converting his 12 roomed house into a fourth. He has sealed the floor-boards, built a wheel-house and stored hun-dreds of pieces of foam for buoyancy. It is already occupied by local cats, pigeons, and a rat.

**WHAT A Joke**

**Baby penguin:** Are you sure I'm a penguin?

**Mother penguin:** Why do you ask?

**Baby penguin:** Because I'm freezing.

Why do policemen carry radios?

**Because radios can't walk.**

Knock, knock.

*Who's there?*

**Wenceslas.**

*Wenceslas who?*

**Wenceslas bus - I wan't to get home.**

**Are you sure you're a qualified glazier?**

What do you call five bottles of lemonade?

**A pop group.**

What happened to the egg in a monastery?

**It went out of the pan and into the friar.**

How does a skeleton ring up his friends?

**On a telebone.**